CARING FOR YOUR

Contents

Introduction 2
Dogs 3
Cats 11
Rabbits 18
Guinea Pigs 26
Hamsters 33
Budgerigars 40
Goldfish 46
Chameleons 52
Stick Insects 57
Useful Addresses and Index 63

Written by Gill Matthews
Illustrated by Debbie Clark

Collins Educational
An imprint of HarperCollins*Publishers*

INTRODUCTION

For thousands of years people all over the world have kept many different animals as pets. They often provide company for their owners and are interesting to study and observe.

You may already own a pet yourself or you may have one at school. This book tells you how to care for pets, both common and more unusual, what they eat, how to keep them clean and how they breed.

Looking after any pet requires time. They will need caring for every day of their lives, and in some cases this could be until you are an adult, so make sure that you have enough spare time to give. Remember that if you go away on holiday, your pet must still be fed, exercised and cleaned.

Pets also cost money. Some are more expensive than others but all will need money spent on them at some time. Make certain you can afford to look after a pet before you get it.

Some pets take up a lot of room. If you live in a flat without a garden then a hamster is a more suitable pet than a large dog that needs plenty of exercise.

Do not allow a pet to breed unless you already have a good home for the young. Never get a pet without asking permission from the adults you live with.

Dogs

Like wolves, jackals and foxes, dogs belong to the carnivorous *canid* family. All domestic dogs are descendants of the wolf and were first tamed over 12,000 years ago. The ancient Egyptians are thought to have been the first people to breed certain types of dogs, which they used for sport, hunting, herding, as guard dogs and for company.

Dogs vary greatly in size and temperament. Over the years, breeders have developed dogs with certain characteristics — these purebreds (pedigree breeds) have ancestors of the same breed. Crossbreds have parents of two different breeds, whilst mongrels have a very mixed, often unknown, ancestry.

Dogs have highly developed senses of smell, sight and sound, although in some purebreds their breeding has developed one particular sense more than the others. The greyhound, for example, has better sight than its ancestor

The Golden Retriever is a popular pedigree breed.

the wolf, whereas beagles have been bred for tracking and their noses are more powerful than their eyes or ears.

Dogs make very affectionate and intelligent pets and they are easier to train than most other animals. They vary greatly in size and temperament and in the amount of exercise needed. The life expectancy of a healthy dog is ten to 18 years, depending on the breed. Small dogs generally live longer than large ones.

Mongrels are often playful, lively animals.

GETTING READY

There are a number of things to consider before acquiring a dog. The breed or size of dog that you choose should depend on where you live: larger dogs need more room and more exercise than small ones. You will need time to take the dog for a walk and to feed and groom it, you also need to think about what you will do with it if you go away on holiday: putting a dog in kennels can be expensive. There is also the cost of feeding and visiting the vet to think about. Dogs like company and will soon become lonely if left alone for more than a few hours, so if your house is empty all day, a dog is not the right pet to choose.

BEDDING

A dog needs its own bed. Puppies tend to chew anything and everything, so a beanbag type of bed will not be suitable. A plastic bed or a wicker basket is a better choice. Line the bed with newspaper and a blanket or an old jumper. Remember that a puppy will grow, so the bed needs to be big enough to take an adult dog. Until the dog is fully grown, it could make do with a cardboard box, again lined with newspaper and a blanket. Replace the box if it becomes dirty or damaged. The bed should be out of draughts, in a warm place, but not right next to a radiator or boiler.

FEEDING AND GROOMING EQUIPMENT

You will need:
- food bowl
- water bowl
- serving spoon and fork
- bristle brush (for short-haired dogs)
- two-sided wire and bristle brush (for long-haired dogs)
- blunt-ended scissors
- comb
- rubber grooming glove
- towel

Other items:
- plenty of old newspaper until the puppy is completely house-trained
- sturdy rubber or plastic toys such as balls or bones

A dog does not need a collar and lead until it is three months old, but the sooner you introduce one, the sooner it will get used to it. By law, a dog must wear an identity disc marked with the owner's name and address.

CHOOSING A DOG

If you want a purebred dog you will have to visit a specialist breeder, or look in dog magazines. Always make sure that you see the mother with her puppies. For crossbreds, you may know of someone who has puppies available or you could enquire at the local vet's surgery. Alternatively, animal sanctuaries and shelters have puppies and adult dogs who need homes. It is best to buy a puppy as an adult dog may have been ill-treated and have problems with people, or have bad habits that are difficult to break. A puppy is ready to leave its mother from about two months old.

Look for a puppy that:
- is alert and playful
- is the sex that you have decided on
- has clear, bright eyes
- has a clean coat
- has clean ears

Ask the owner:
- what food it eats, how much and how often
- whether it has been vaccinated, if so there will be a certificate of vaccination
- whether it has been treated for worms
- if it is partly house-trained
- for the pedigree certificate (if it is a purebred)

GOING HOME

If you are travelling by car you can carry the puppy in your arms; it may feel more secure wrapped in a blanket. On a long journey you will need a drinking bowl and water, also a supply of newspaper in case of accidents. If you need to stop, do not leave the puppy alone in the car with the windows closed for a long period of time.

Until the puppy has completed its first course of injections at about three months, it cannot be allowed to walk on the streets, as it could pick up infections from other dogs. So, if you are walking home or travelling by public transport, you will either have to carry the dog in your arms or use a carrying box.

Once home, show the puppy its bed, give it something to eat and drink and allow it to explore its new surroundings. For the first few nights it may feel lonely and cry – a warm hot water bottle and a ticking clock in its bed will help.

If you have other pets, never leave them alone with a new puppy until you are sure how they will react to each other. Make a fuss of your other dogs or cats so that they don't feel left out or ignored.

HOUSE-TRAINING

A puppy can generally be house-trained by six months old, however it does take time and patience. Never punish it for going to the toilet in the wrong place but give plenty of praise when it uses the right place.

Spread sheets of newspaper in one area on the floor. When the puppy wants to go to the toilet it will probably start whimpering, sniffing the floor and turning round in circles. Take the puppy to the paper, hold it there gently until it has finished and then praise it.

If you have a garden, take the puppy out first thing in the morning and after it has eaten. You will find that it starts to bark and scratch at the door when it needs to go out.

If it goes to the toilet indoors, wash and disinfect the floor and rinse it with vinegar and water, the smell will put the puppy off using the same place again.

If you do not have a garden house-training will take longer, as the puppy cannot go outside until fully vaccinated. After three months, take it out on a lead. Never allow your dog to foul the pavement. You can buy disposable scoops and plastic bags for clearing up after it. Some parks have special dog toilet areas that dogs can use before being allowed off the lead.

FEEDING

The amount of food a puppy needs depends very much on its size. Start with a saucerful – if it eats that in one go and still appears to be hungry, offer a little more. Have a bowl of clean water available at all times. Until it is four months old it will need four meals a day; the content will depend on the breeder's recommendation but may be a little dry baby cereal mixed with milk for breakfast and supper; and tinned puppy food mixed with an equal amount of dog meal softened in gravy, water or milk at midday and again during the afternoon. At four months, drop the morning feed and give the midday feed earlier. At six months, drop the last feed and move the afternoon feed to the evening. At nine months, feed as an adult, giving all the food at one meal, preferably in the evening. Very small dogs continue to need two feeds, one in the morning and one in the evening.

Adult dogs' requirements vary according to size and appetite. They should be fed on a reputable good-quality canned or dry dog food to ensure all the nutrients are present in the correct balance. Dogs need to chew to keep their teeth and gums healthy, but never give them chicken, lamb or chop bones as they can splinter and cut the dog's mouth or get stuck in the throat. It is possible to buy hide chews for dogs from pet shops.

TRAINING

Start to train the puppy once it is used to wearing a collar and walking on the lead. Make sure that the collar is not too tight and that the puppy cannot squeeze its head out. You should be able to slip two fingers between the collar and the puppy's neck. To get it accustomed to the lead, start by walking it around the house or garden.

The first commands to concentrate on are 'heel', 'sit', 'stay' and 'come'. You can later train your dog to retrieve and carry.

Always use the same command words or the puppy will become confused; also use its name. You must be kind but firm when you are training; always praise and never punish. Ten minutes training a day will be enough for a puppy.

Look locally for dog-training classes or visit the library to find specialist books on training dogs.

GROOMING

The amount of grooming a dog needs depends on the length of its coat.

Long-haired dogs need grooming every day.
- Use a wire brush to separate the hair, be careful not to scratch the skin.
- Brush the whole coat with the wire brush.
- Using a bristle brush, brush the coat in the direction that the coat grows (generally from the head towards the tail).
- Cut away any matted hair with blunt-ended scissors.

Short-haired dogs need to be groomed once a week.
- Use a bristle brush to groom the whole coat.
- Remove loose hair with a rubber grooming glove.

Whilst grooming the dog check that the ears are clean, there are no bare patches on the coat and that the claws are not split or too long.

Generally dogs only need bathing three or four times a year, unless they get dirty or are light-coloured. Always dry a dog as quickly as possible after its bath.

BREEDING

You will need to think very carefully about what to do with the puppies before allowing a female dog (bitch) to become pregnant. Although she will probably give birth without any assistance, you will need adult help with caring for the puppies.

Many dog owners decide to have their dogs neutered to prevent them from breeding. Unneutered males tend to wander, looking for a mate, and can become restless and bad-tempered if they are prevented from mating. Unneutered bitches come into 'season' twice a year, when they can become pregnant. Whilst they do not get the urge to wander off, they will attract local males. Bitches can be neutered or 'spayed' between seven months and one year old.

If you decide to breed from your purebred dog, you will need to look for a mate of the same breed. You can write to the Kennel Club for a list of breeders (see Useful Addresses, p 63) or check advertisements in dog magazines.

The most suitable age for a bitch to have her first litter is around 18 months. If your bitch becomes pregnant, take her to the vet for a check-up and again soon before the puppies are due to be born. In the second month of pregnancy she will need three times the amount of food, and may need a mineral and vitamin supplement. The pregnancy will last for about nine weeks. Small dogs tend to have litters of between one and six puppies, whereas larger dogs have litters of five to twelve.

Ten days after the puppies are born their eyes will open, and they can start to be weaned off their mother's milk at four weeks. They will be ready to leave their mother when they are eight to ten weeks old. The mother and her litter should be taken to the vet for a check-up about three weeks after the birth.

HEALTH

If well cared for, your dog should lead a long and healthy life. If its behaviour changes, visit your vet.

CATS

Cats belong to the *felid* family, as do lions, tigers and pumas. Domestic cats still retain certain instincts of wildcats, in that they will hunt and climb trees. European wildcats are fairly timid but the North African breed is bolder. It is thought that the ancient Egyptians first tamed the North African wildcat over 5,000 years ago, when they were used to control the numbers of rats and mice on farms. Egyptian traders carried cats on board their ships and so introduced them into Europe.

Cats are one of the most popular pets all over the world. Crossbreds tend to have a round head with a wide face and small

Cats make ideal house pets as they do not take up much room and are quite self-sufficient.

pointed ears. They have a variety of coloured and patterned coats with fur of differing lengths. They have keen senses of smell, sight and hearing and an amazing ability to fall on their feet from great heights, known as the 'righting reflex'.

Male cats can live for 12 to 15 years, females a couple of years longer, although it has been known for cats to live for 20 or even 30 years.

GETTING READY

Cats do not take up a lot of room. Whilst they like the warmth and comfort of a house, they also enjoy being outdoors where they can exercise and play. However, if you are thinking about having a cat as a pet, do remember that it is a long-term commitment. The cost of feeding and health care must be considered, also that you will need time to groom and feed them every day.

BEDDING

Providing your cat with a bed will ensure it sleeps there rather than on the furniture. It can be a wicker basket, a plastic box, a beanbag or just a cardboard box lined with newspaper. The bed should have a washable lining and be large enough for the cat to be able to stretch out.

Make sure that the bed is not in a draught. If the cat doesn't like the position of its bed it won't use it, so you may have to experiment. As cats spend about 16 hours a day asleep, the bed is an important piece of equipment.

You will also need a plastic or metal mesh carrying box, not only for bringing your cat home, but also for trips to the vet.

LITTER TRAY

If you are getting a kitten, or if your cat will be spending long periods of time indoors, it will need a litter tray. Line it with old newspaper or litter liners and spread a layer of cat litter 5-6cm deep on the top. Keep it well away from where your cat eats and sleeps.

CAT FLAP

These need to be fitted in a back or side door by an adult. They allow a cat to come and go as it pleases, if it is going to be left alone during the day. For security they can be locked at night. One drawback to cat flaps is that neighbourhood cats will also use them, so you may find that you have visitors, unless you buy one with a magnetic lock.

If your cat is going to roam, it is a good idea to fit a collar with an identity disc printed with your name and address. The collar should be elasticated so that if it becomes caught, the cat can wriggle out of it.

FEEDING AND GROOMING EQUIPMENT

You will need:
- food bowl
- water bowl
- spoon and fork
- brush
- comb
- toys

CHOOSING A CAT

Animal shelters are a good place to start looking for a cat. Both kittens and adult cats are usually available. You may know of someone whose cat is expecting a litter of kittens or you could look in the local newspaper adverts. For purebred (pedigree) cats you will need to contact a breeder.

Kittens should be between eight and nine weeks old before they leave their mother. Try to see the whole litter together with the mother.

Look for a kitten that:
- is lively and friendly
- is the sex that you have decided on

- has bright eyes and a clean nose
- has a pale pink mouth with clean white teeth
- has a clean coat (check under the tail)

Ask the owner which injections the kitten has had, what food it prefers and how often it eats.

GOING HOME

Take the carrying box into the room containing the cat's bed, making sure that the windows and doors are securely closed. Don't forget a litter tray. Allow the kitten to explore the room, show it the litter tray and bed.

If you have other cats or a dog, introduce them to each other but do not leave them alone until they are used to each other.

Once the kitten is used to the room it can gradually be allowed to explore the rest of the house.

HOLIDAYS

If you are going away you will need to ask a friend or neighbour to look after your cat. Leave a list of food it eats, the quantity and how often it should be fed. Also leave the phone number of the vet.

If you cannot find anyone to care for your cat, you can take it to a cattery.

HOUSE-TRAINING

Kittens will often have been trained by their mother to use a litter tray. If your cat is not house-trained, put it into the litter tray every half hour. It will soon realise what it is for. If the cat refuses to use the litter tray check that the tray is clean and does not smell of other cats.

Your cat needs to keep its claws trimmed and to strip off the worn claw sheaths. It does this by scratching. It is also marking its territory as glands behind the claws leave a scent. When a cat is young it does not realise that clawing the furniture will not be popular, but it is important to stop this behaviour as soon as possible. Firmly tell your cat 'no' and remove it from where it is scratching. If the cat is not able to go outside to scratch, you may need to provide a piece of wood for it to use.

FEEDING

Cats are meat eaters (carnivores). Adult cats need two meals a day, kittens eat more often. Always feed the cat in the same place and at the same time every day, as they are creatures of habit.

Your cat will need two bowls; one for food and one for water. Set aside a spoon and fork purely for serving the cat's food. Never use bowls or cutlery that the rest of the family eat from and always wash the cat's bowls separately.

For an occasional treat, you may want to give your cat fresh meat. It is best to serve this cooked rather than raw. To ensure that the cat is getting all the nourishment it needs, use ready prepared cat food, available from pet shops and supermarkets. These come in three forms – moist, semi-dry and dry. Read the label to find out how much to serve; the amount does depend on the age and size of the cat. Moist food should be removed after half an hour as it goes stale quickly; dry food can be left for longer.

Always have a bowl of fresh water available for your cat, particularly if it has dry food. Giving a cat your leftovers can upset its stomach. Never give it bones as it could choke on the splinters.

GROOMING

Cats are very clean creatures and will groom themselves regularly. Your cat will use its paws and saliva to wash its face and the rough surface of its tongue to 'comb' its fur. Dirt and small twigs are removed with its teeth.

Even short-haired cats need regular grooming. They must be

brushed to prevent them swallowing a lot of fur, which can cause fur balls to form in the stomach. Long-haired cats should be groomed daily. Use a wide-toothed comb and brush from head to tail, carefully untangling any knots with your fingers.

BEHAVIOUR

If you watch a kitten when it is playing you will see it practising stalking and hunting skills. You can make toys and join in with these games. Cats' toys do not have to be expensive and complicated. Kittens will chase a ball of paper or wool across the floor; hang a cotton reel on a piece of elastic from a door handle and they will strike at it with their paws.

Your cat will miaow to attract attention and you will soon start to recognise its different calls. It will purr when it is contented but also if it is in pain. When a cat is angry it waves its tail slowly and makes a low grumbling sound in its throat. If your cat is irritated, leave it alone. A cat's ears indicate its mood; they are normally erect and alert. If a cat is about to attack its ears move back and down, when they are completely flat it is defensive.

An angry cat arches its back, its hair stands on end, the pupils will become narrow slits and it will hiss. The cat is trying to make itself appear as large as possible to frighten whatever is threatening it.

A cat will often greet you by rubbing against your legs. Although this is a friendly gesture, it is also marking you with its scent. Cats are very territorial creatures and will mark their patch outdoors in this way. They also do this by spraying urine, leaving behind an extremely strong and unpleasant smell.

BREEDING

Unless you wish to breed from your cat, it is advisable to have it neutered at the age of five or six months. This will mean that female cats will not be able to have kittens and that males will be less inclined to wander off or fight, and they will certainly be less smelly.

If you do decide to breed from your cat, think very carefully about what you will do with the kittens. Female cats (queens), usually give birth with very little trouble after a pregnancy lasting about nine weeks. A litter normally consists of three to five kittens. They are born blind and deaf. After about ten days their eyes open, after two weeks their teeth start to grow, at three weeks they start to explore and at four weeks they can be handled. From four weeks they can start to be weaned off their mother's milk; weaning will be completed by the time they are eight weeks old.

HEALTH
Do the following health check once a week:
- coat – should feel dry and smell clean, check for parasites and fleas
- paws – make sure the pads are undamaged and that nothing is stuck between them, claws should not be too long
- ears – clean and odourless
- eyes – bright and shiny, no discharge in the corners
- mouth – nothing stuck inside, pink tongue and clean teeth
- behaviour – active and lively
- diet – interested in food

If you think that your cat is unwell, take it to the vet for a health check.

From the age of two months a cat should be vaccinated annually against cat flu, feline infectious enteritis and feline leukemia. All of these diseases can be fatal.

RABBITS

Rabbits are lagomorphs, meaning 'like hares'. They have a similar body shape to hares but with shorter back legs and ears. They have been kept as domestic animals in Europe since the Roman times and were introduced into Britain by the Normans, who farmed them for food.

Domestic rabbits are descendants of wild European rabbits and, like them, are more active in the evening than during the day.

They have sharp front teeth which do not stop growing and are used for gnawing; they also have very keen senses of smell, sight and hearing. When alarmed, they hold up their tail or 'scut', showing the white underside, to warn other rabbits of danger.

Rabbits make delightful pets for younger children.

Domestic rabbits vary widely in size, from the dwarf breeds like the Netherland Dwarf, which may only weigh 1kg, to the giant breeds like the Belgian Hare and Flemish Giant, which can weigh as much as 5kg. Their ears also vary. They can be upright or floppy, as with the lop-eared breeds. Lop-eared rabbits do not have as good a sense of hearing as those with upright ears. Most domestic rabbits have short coats, approximately 2-3cm long, although breeders have developed varieties with fluffy, velvety, even curly coats. They can be speckled, like those of wild rabbits, all one colour or in patterns of two or more colours.

Crossbred rabbits – a mix of breeds, are readily available from pet shops and make ideal pets. They are easy to look after, friendly and their food is relatively inexpensive. There are over 100 pure breeds of rabbits, and it is advisable to purchase these direct from specialist breeders.

A well cared for rabbit may live for six to eight years, if not longer.

HOUSING

Rabbits are very active animals so they must have plenty of space. Ready-made hutches are sold in pet shops but you may know someone who will make one for you. A hutch measuring 120cm wide x 60cm deep will be big enough for one small rabbit.

Rabbit hutch

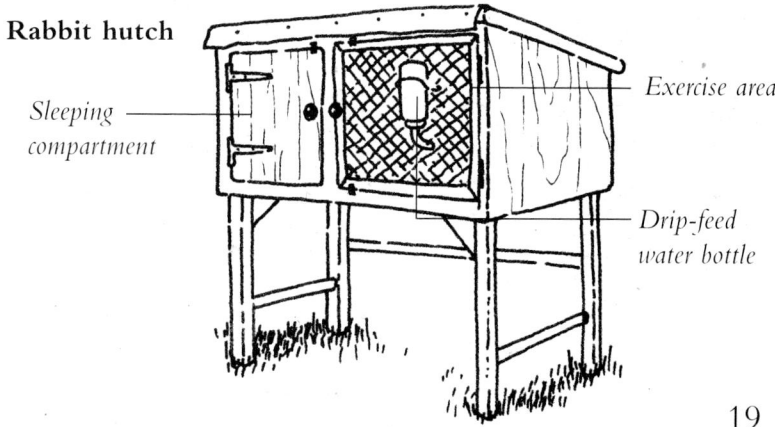

Sleeping compartment

Exercise area

Drip-feed water bottle

When choosing or designing a hutch, remember the following points:
- the roof should be covered in roofing felt or some other waterproof material
- the roof should slope and overhang the sides of the hutch slightly to allow rainwater to run off
- there should be two compartments; an exercise area with a wire mesh front to allow air to circulate, and a sleeping area with a solid wooden door to keep out draughts
- the hutch should either be on legs or on a table to avoid the risk of flooding and keep it out of the reach of other animals
- the doors should have secure bolts
- the hutch must be escape-proof and easy to clean

Rabbits can tolerate the cold but not draughts, damp or hot, stuffy conditions, so think carefully about the position of the hutch. It should be in a dry, sheltered area, safe from other animals such as cats. If the hutch is in a shed or garage, make sure the rabbit gets plenty of air and natural light.

Before collecting the rabbit you will need to prepare the hutch: line the floor with old newspaper and spread wood shavings on top of it, place straw in the sleeping area.

FEEDING EQUIPMENT
You will need:
- hayrack screwed to one of the wooden walls
- heavy pottery dish for food
- gravity-feed water bottle fastened to the wire mesh
- salt lick
- gnawing log, preferably a small branch from a fruit tree

CLEANING AND GROOMING EQUIPMENT
Keep any equipment for cleaning out the hutch separate from household cleaning materials.

You will need:
- rubber gloves
- dustpan and brush
- paint scraper
- bucket and scrubbing brush
- detergent and disinfectant (check with a vet which are suitable)
- bottle brush
- baby's hairbrush

OUTDOORS

During the spring and summer, you can put your rabbit in a Mordant run, also known as an ark, on a lawn or grassy area. This is a triangular-shaped wooden frame, covered in wire mesh and with a wire mesh floor to prevent the rabbit from burrowing. Some Mordant runs also have enclosed sleeping compartments. Do check that the grass has not been treated with weedkiller or other chemicals and that there are no poisonous plants (see p 22-23).

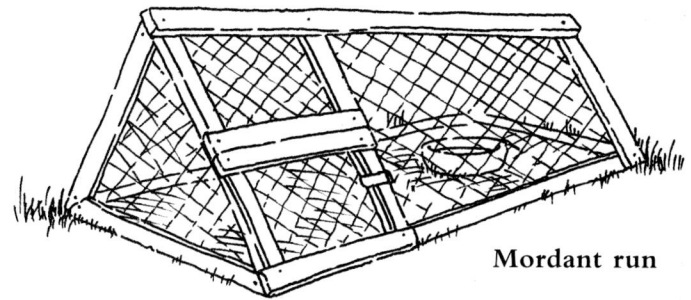
Mordant run

The Mordant run should be moved every few days, although you will need help with this as they are quite heavy. Remember to remove any droppings from the lawn.

CHOOSING A RABBIT

Young rabbits, also known as kittens, should be at least six weeks old before being taken away from their mother. It is best to wait until the warmer months as the move from a warm nest to a colder hutch is quite a shock to a young rabbit. Ideally, check the size of the kitten's parents, to give you an idea of how big your rabbit will grow.

Look for a rabbit that has:

- bright, clean eyes
- a clean, dry nose
- clean, alert ears (except for Lops)
- soft, dry fur
- an inquisitive, lively nature

If you are planning to keep more than one rabbit, it is best to choose two females (does). You will need a carrying box to bring your rabbit home. A cat's travelling box is ideal.

FEEDING

Rabbits are herbivores. In the wild they eat seeds, roots and wild grasses. Pet rabbits will happily graze on grass and eat dried grass or hay, but they also need special rabbit food in the form of a mix or pellets. These contain a mixture of dried plants, seeds and vegetables.

Feed your rabbit both in the morning and evening, cleaning the food bowl well before filling it with food. Rabbits eat as

Safe Plants

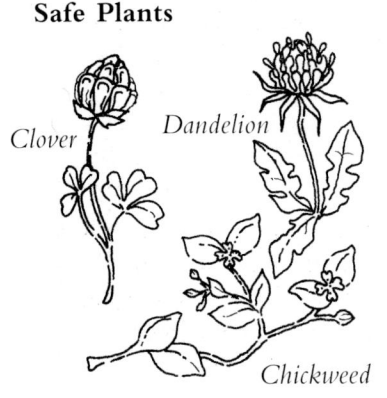

Clover

Dandelion

Chickweed

Poisonous Plants

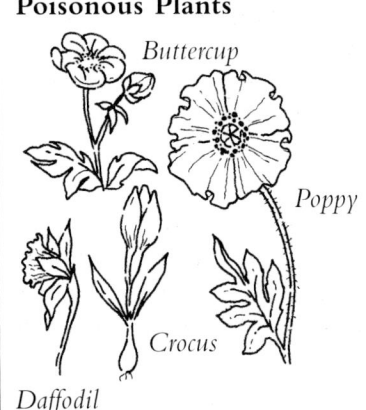

Buttercup

Poppy

Crocus

Daffodil

much as they need and should not become overweight if they have exercise.

Wild plants such as dandelions, chickweed, clover and shepherd's purse are all suitable for rabbits. Certain plants are poisonous: bulb plants such as daffodils and crocuses; poppies and buttercups. If in any doubt about a plant, do not give it to your rabbit.

A handful of washed, fresh fruit such as apples, tomatoes and melon and clean, chopped vegetables such as celery, peas, cabbage, carrots, lettuce and cucumber can be given to the rabbit as part of its evening feed. Give very small quantities at first, as some rabbits may get digestive upsets. It is important to keep the water bottle full and clean. Rabbits need a constant supply of water as the food makes them thirsty.

CLEANING THE HUTCH

Always wash your hands before and after cleaning the hutch and grooming the rabbit. Check the hutch daily and remove uneaten food. Rabbits tend to use one corner of the hutch for their droppings – clean this area every day.

The hutch should be cleaned at least once a week, more often in hot weather. Wear rubber gloves when cleaning out the hutch. Remove used litter and bedding. Using a paint scraper, scrape off anything stuck to the floor. Pay particular attention to the corners. Sweep out the hutch with a dustpan and brush. Scrub with hot soapy water, rinse and spray with a disinfectant. Allow to dry completely. Clean and refill the water bottle. Replace litter and bedding.

GROOMING

Rabbits do groom themselves but you can help by brushing them each day. If you have a long-haired breed like Cashmere or Angora, their fur tends to become tangled, so a daily grooming session is even more important. Brush away from the head towards the tail, tackling the back, underneath and under the chin.

Whilst grooming, check the length of your rabbit's claws. They can be clipped by a vet if they become too long.

BREEDING

Before allowing a doe to have kittens, think carefully about what you will do with them once they are born. You might find that your local pet shop is willing to take them, or you may have friends who would like their own rabbits. Rabbits should not be mated until they are at least six or seven months old. The best time of year is in the warmer months of spring or early summer. It is possible to mate different breeds as long as they are a similar size.

Always take the doe to the buck's hutch. Stand by with a pair of sturdy gloves as they may start to fight – if they do, remove the doe and return her to her hutch. Mating takes place fairly quickly and you may find that the buck falls over onto his side afterwards for a short time. Remove the doe and take her back to her own hutch.

How to tell if your rabbit is a buck or a doe

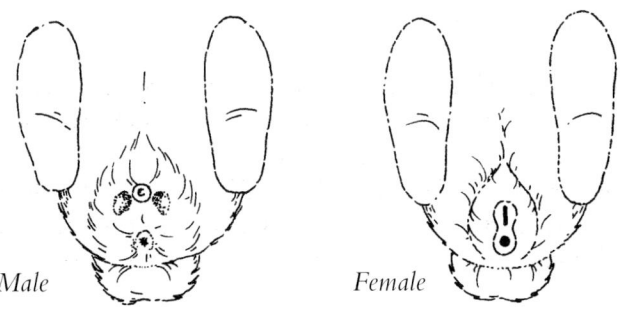

Male　　　　　　　　Female

The doe will require a larger hutch for her kittens and herself, or a nesting box with one low side for access into the hutch. The gestation period between mating and giving birth (kindling) is about 31 days. After about 25 days the doe starts to prepare her nest, lining it with fur. She needs plenty of nourishment at this stage and will be very thirsty, so always provide a good supply of drinking water. About a day before she gives birth she may go off her food.

A litter can number anything between one and ten kittens; they are born blind, deaf and without fur. It is important not to disturb them for the first day.

On the second day check the litter, then leave them alone. It is possible that one or more of the kittens will be born dead. If this is the case, remove the bodies and dispose of them safely.

For the first three weeks of their lives the kittens feed on their mother's milk, so the doe needs extra food and water at this time. They grow quickly: by the fourth day they start to grow fur and after ten days their eyes are open. After about two and a half weeks they start to leave the nesting box and move around the cage.

At four to six weeks the kittens will try food that is available in the hutch and at eight weeks they can be taken away from the doe, either into their own hutch or to their new owners. At 12 weeks males and females should be housed separately.

HEALTH

The most serious disease that affects rabbits is myxomatosis, which is spread by fleas. There is no cure, although you can ask the vet to vaccinate your rabbit against it.

Rabbits can also suffer from 'the snuffles'; the signs to look for are runny eyes and nose, sneezing and a cough. It is similar to a cold and is infectious, so always move a sick rabbit into a separate hutch.

If your rabbit's front teeth become too long, put a gnawing log into the hutch. Alternatively, your vet will file them down. In the wild, rabbits keep their claws short by burrowing.

GUINEA PIGS

Guinea pigs are friendly, inquisitive creatures.

Despite their name, guinea pigs are not pigs but rodents. They belong to the *caviidae* family and are descendants of the Tschudi guinea pig of Chile. In the wild, they live in colonies of between five and ten, spending most of their time grazing for food. They are very sociable, non-aggressive animals. Because they are defenceless creatures, they can move quickly and are very agile.

Guinea pigs are thought to have been in existence for 35 to 40 million years. They were first domesticated 5,000 – 11,000 years ago, when they were bred for food. In 1670, Dutch merchants brought the animals back to Holland from Central and Southern America as pets. Ten years later they were being sold in France and the UK, although at the time they were expensive and could only be afforded by the very wealthy. Emigrants from the UK took guinea pigs to the USA in the early 18th century.

The different breeds are mainly determined by the lengths of their coats, which are short, rough or long (long-haired breeds can have fur of 15-20cm in length). They can be one colour (known as self-coloured), two colours or more.

A healthy guinea pig can live for up to eight years.

GETTING READY

As guinea pigs enjoy company, keeping them in suitable pairings is ideal. Ready-made hutches are available from pet shops, although you may know someone who could make one for you. A hutch for two animals should measure at least 150 x 60 x 60cm and be divided into two sections, for day and night use. The day section should have a wire mesh front to allow in light and air, the night section should have a solid wood front for protection. Ideally the two sections should have separate doors.

The hutch should be raised off the ground to avoid damp and make it easier to clean out, and have a sloping roof which

Guinea pig hutch

Daytime area

Sleeping compartment

Drip-feed water bottle

overhangs the sides. The hutch bottom should be covered with a layer of newspaper and wood shavings. Use hay or oat straw in the bedding area. Never leave the hutch outside at night as guinea pigs dislike the cold. A Mordant run (see p 21) could be used if the weather is warm. Make sure that there is a covered area to give the animals some shelter. On very sunny days, position the Mordant run in the shade as guinea pigs can become overheated.

FEEDING EQUIPMENT
You will need:
- food bowl – this should be a heavy earthenware dish that cannot be knocked over
- gravity-feed water bottle with a metal spout
- mineral lick
- hayrack

CLEANING AND GROOMING EQUIPMENT
Keep any equipment for cleaning out the hutch separate from household cleaning materials.
You will need:
- rubber gloves
- dustpan and brush
- paint scraper
- bucket and scrubbing brush
- detergent and disinfectant (check with the vet which are suitable)
- bottle brush
- baby's hairbrush (for long-haired breeds)

CHOOSING A GUINEA PIG
If you want a pedigree guinea pig to show, visit a breeder. Contact the National Cavy Club for details of local breeders (see Useful Addresses, p 63).

Most pet shops stock crossbred guinea pigs. Once a young guinea pig is weaned it can be taken away from its mother, so look for an animal aged between six and 12 weeks. Do bear in mind that if a female is older than two months she may already be pregnant.

Look for a guinea pig that:
- is alert and active
- has a good appetite
- has trim, clean teeth
- has clean eyes, nose and mouth
- has a firm, plump body
- has short, undamaged claws
- breathes quietly and easily

Check the sexes if you buy a pair; a male and a female will mate, two males may fight, whereas two females will live happily.

FEEDING

Guinea pigs are very easy to feed although they tend to be messy eaters. Food and fresh water should always be available. Their daily requirements are: fresh grass or hay; fresh vegetables and grain or cereals.

Put the grass or hay in the hayrack, making sure it is clear of the floor. For vitamin C, give your guinea pig washed fruit and vegetables such as celery, apples, tomatoes or melon; do not give potato peelings or raw beans. You can also give it wild plants such as dandelions, cow parsley, vetch, nettles and clover. Bindweed, dock leaves and ragwort are poisonous to guinea pigs.

Pet shops sell a ready-prepared grain mix. Be sure to buy one especially for guinea pigs, not rabbits, as the vitamin C content is important. Cereals can be added in the form of oats, wholemeal bread or bran, given dry or mixed with milk or water. Guinea pigs eat as much as they need during a day (about one or two tablespoons of grain mix). If they regularly leave food, serve them less.

For gnawing, put hard bread, crackers, nibbling sticks (available from pet shops) and small branches into the cage. A salt or mineral lick can be hung on the side of the cage.

Always feed the guinea pig at the same time each day and remove any food that is left after one hour (except for the hay).

CLEANING THE HUTCH

Whilst you are cleaning out the guinea pig's hutch, put it into a large open-topped box containing some hay.

Each day, remove any droppings and damp bedding, replacing the bedding with clean hay or straw.

The hutch will need completely cleaning out once a week. Remove all of the bedding, newspaper and wood shavings. Scrape the floor of the hutch with a paint scraper, paying particular attention to the corners. Wipe the hutch out with a mixture of disinfectant and water. Once it is completely dry, replace the newspaper and shavings and put new bedding in the night area. Always wash your hands after cleaning the cage.

GROOMING

Long and rough-haired guinea pigs will need grooming once a day, short-haired breeds once a week. Hold the guinea pig firmly on your lap or on a table. Using a soft brush, always brush in the direction that the fur grows. Remove any droppings that are stuck to the coat. A guinea pig will only need bathing if it is very dirty or going to be shown. Use a special pet shampoo and keep it indoors until it is completely dry.

Whilst grooming your pet, check the condition of its coat, teeth and claws.

HANDLING

Guinea pigs are easy to handle and will soon become used to it. Do take care not to drop them as their bones might break.

How to handle a guinea pig

Always approach from the front when you are going to pick a guinea pig up, so that it is not taken by surprise. With a young guinea pig, cup one hand over its shoulders, supporting its weight, with your other hand beneath its hindquarters. An adult animal should be held in a similar way, but with one hand under the chest, rather than over the shoulders.

BREEDING

A female guinea pig (sow) can produce five litters a year, as guinea pigs can mate every 14 to 18 days. The best age to breed from a guinea pig is six months to two years. Pregnancy lasts from eight to ten weeks. After about four weeks the female starts to look fatter. She will need extra food and water whilst she is pregnant. Guinea pigs give birth easily. The young are born fully developed with open eyes and thick fur, weighing 40-100g. They are able to move quickly and eat solid food straightaway as they are born with teeth; however, they will take their mother's milk for the first two or three weeks.

Females are ready to mate at five to six weeks, males at nine to ten weeks, so they should be kept separately from that age.

How to tell the sex of a guinea pig

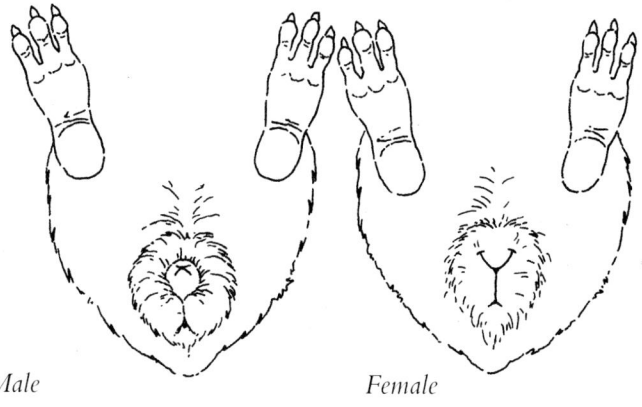

Male *Female*

HEALTH

There are a number of health risks to watch out for. If any of these occur, take your guinea pig to the vet for advice and treatment:
- heatstroke – guinea pigs should be kept in the shade if outside in warm weather, as they can become overheated
- colds – if your pet becomes wheezy and appears to be having breathing problems, it may have a chest infection or even pneumonia
- diarrhoea – this can be caused by a change in diet or an infection
- ringworm – symptoms are bald patches in the fur. Ringworm can be caught by humans. Always keep the hutch clean and wash your hands after handling your pet
- skin problems – parasites cause itchy sore spots but can be treated with anti-parasitic shampoo
- flystrike – flies will lay their eggs on droppings stuck to the guinea pig's coat. The maggots that hatch then burrow into the flesh. This can be fatal, so always keep your guinea pig's coat well-groomed
- overweight – this can lead to an early death, so make sure that your pet does not overeat and has plenty of exercise

HAMSTERS

Hamsters are one of the most popular rodent pets. They belong to the *cricetidae* family, along with voles. All hamsters have cheek pouches in which they hold food; their name comes from the German word 'hamster' which means to hoard.

In the wild, hamsters, which are nocturnal animals, are found in desert areas. During the day, whilst it is hot, they sleep underground in burrows and tunnels. At night, when the temperature drops, they emerge from their tunnels to look for food. They eat mainly dry seeds and are thought to travel great distances at night in search of food, which they carry in their cheek pouches, returning to their burrows to put it in their food store. Their eyesight is poor, due to the amount of time they spend in darkness.

The Syrian hamster is a popular breed.

Hamsters were introduced to the UK in 1931 and most of them are the Golden or Syrian hamster. Although they are naturally a golden brown colour with a white underside, there are now over 100 different colours which have been developed through selective breeding.

Hamsters are easily tamed and do not need a lot of attention. They are solitary animals and should be kept singly rather than in pairs or groups. Generally, a hamster will live for between 18 months and two years and males tend to live slightly longer than females.

GETTING READY

Hamsters are well known for their ability to gnaw their way out of captivity, so make sure that the cage is escape-proof. One measuring 75 x 40 x 40cm is ideal. Cages can be bought from pet shops or home-made – if someone is making a cage for you, it should be made from hardwood or a plastic-coated material that is difficult for the hamster to gnaw.

Hamsters have a strong nesting instinct, so provide a nesting box in the cage, filled with soft hay or nesting material. The cage should be designed so that a fairly deep layer of litter can be spread on the floor to enable the hamster to burrow as it would do in the wild. Put a layer of coarse sawdust over the floor, then layers of hay, paper or cardboard (do not use newspapers or magazines as the printing ink may be poisonous). The hamster will then shred and arrange the materials.

A gnawing block should be provided. As a hamster gnaws it wears down its incisors, which, like other rodents, do not stop growing. A piece of hardwood, an unshelled brazil nut, a carrot or dog biscuit are all suitable for gnawing on.

Water should be provided in a drip-feed water bottle as a bowl would soon get knocked over or filled with food and litter. A small, heavy bowl is suitable for food.

It is possible to train a hamster to use a small, shallow plastic

The inside of a hamster's cage should have lots of room for the animal to exercise.

tray containing sawdust as a toilet area. When cleaning it out, leave a small amount of the damp sawdust in the tray – the hamster will use the tray again because of the smell. Hamsters are naturally very active creatures, particularly at night, so they need room to exercise. Ideally, a cage should have a number of different levels or a gallery area so that the hamster can jump from one surface to another. A wheel provides an opportunity for exercise; make sure that it has a solid surface rather than open spokes, as the hamster could get its legs trapped. If it is not fixed close to the cage wall, the hamster could get stuck behind it. Provide a playground area by putting a toilet roll tube, a small branch or climbing frame into the cage.

If you allow your pet out into the room to play, it needs constant supervision as it can jump and climb further than you think. It can also squeeze through very small gaps and may escape into the rest of the house. If this should happen, try tempting it back by leaving some food on the floor.

CHOOSING A HAMSTER

If you want to breed or show a hamster, buy from a breeder, if not, it can be bought from pet shops. Syrian and Golden hamsters must be kept singly as two will fight, but Chinese and Russian hamsters can be kept in pairs. As they are nocturnal animals they can be quite noisy at night, particularly if playing on an exercise wheel. Your pet may not be very active when you are around during the day, although if you offer food during the late afternoon a young hamster may be trained to wake earlier.

Choose a young hamster, aged between five and eight weeks, so that it will become used to being handled and be easier to tame. Only buy a long-haired hamster if you have time for regular grooming.

Look for a hamster that:
- has a plump body shape
- has soft, glossy fur
- has clean skin, without sores or abcesses
- has no dampness under the tail

GOING HOME

Take your hamster home in a secure, well-ventilated box containing hay or paper. Allow it to run from the box into the cage, provide some food and water and leave it undisturbed for 24 hours to settle down.

FEEDING

Hamsters eat seeds, grains and nuts: pre-packed food is available from pet shops. Wash fresh fruit and vegetables such as apples, pears, tomatoes, salad vegetables, cabbage, carrots and swede before

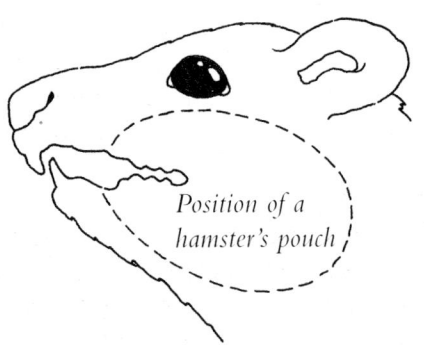

Position of a hamster's pouch

giving them to the hamster. Wild plants like clover, dandelion and groundsel are suitable, but do make sure that they have not been sprayed with any chemicals and do not collect them from the roadside. Coltsfoot, rhubarb, potato and tomato leaves are all poisonous to hamsters. Occasionally, offer your hamster protein in the form of small quantities of sliced hard-boiled egg, cheese, cooked flakes of fish and meat.

You should feed the hamster once a day in the late afternoon or early evening. One heaped teaspoon of seeds and grains should be sufficient, although do supply slightly more so that it can pouch and then store some food. Fresh fruit, vegetables or greenstuff can be given later in the evening or early morning – only give as much as the hamster will eat in one day. If, when you are putting food into the cage you tap lightly on the side, the hamster will soon associate the sound with food. Hamsters do not eat very large quantities and will store what they do not eat. Clear away any uneaten perishable food from the foodstore on a daily basis as it will soon rot and start to smell.

CLEANING AND GROOMING

Each day, clear away any droppings from the cage, and empty and clean the toilet tray. Refill the water bottle, check that there is enough bedding in the nesting box and that it is clean. The cage should be cleaned thoroughly, once a week, in the way described for rabbits (see p 23).

Short-haired hamsters will groom themselves, whereas long-haired animals will need grooming at least every other day. Use a soft dry toothbrush, brushing from the head towards the tail.

The teeth will be kept clean by gnawing.

HANDLING

A young hamster will need to be tamed and become used to being handled; this should only take a few weeks. Start by stroking it gently and feeding it from your hand, then move on to lifting it by cupping it in your hands. Once it is used to being held, lift it with your finger and thumb on the loose skin on the back of its neck, supporting its body with your other hand.

A hamster will jump if startled or surprised, so always hold it no higher than 20cm above a surface. They can injure themselves if they fall; their delicate bone structure means that broken bones are a risk.

BREEDING

As hamsters should be kept singly, the question of breeding does not normally arise. If you do decide to breed from your hamster, take plenty of advice from an experienced breeder. Female hamsters can be very aggressive and seriously injure a male.

Young hamsters are normally born in litters of five to seven, after a pregnancy of about 16 days. They are born virtually helpless, blind and with little fur. After about 12 days their eyes will open and by four weeks they will be eating solid food and becoming independent. At five or six weeks old they will need to be separated.

How to tell the sex of a hamster

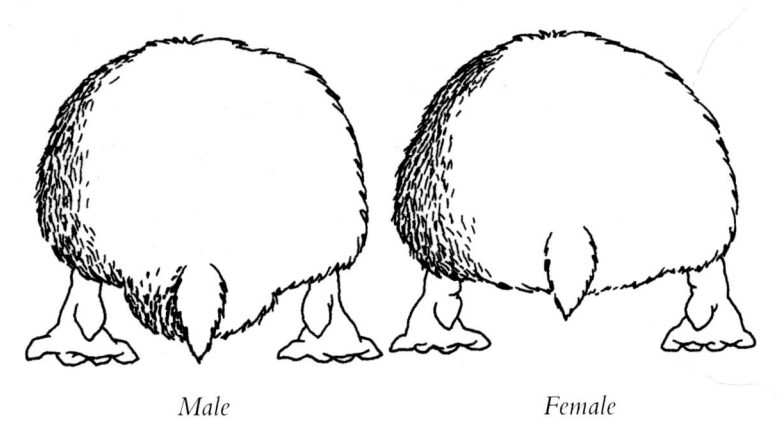

Male *Female*

HEALTH

If a hamster's living conditions and diet are good, it should remain healthy. Handle your pet every day and check its appearance; a healthy hamster will have:
- a good appetite
- alert, quick movements during its active period
- a plump, rounded body with no sores or swellings
- silent, regular breathing
- a clean, dry coat. Hamsters do start to lose their fur with age
- short, undamaged claws
- clean ears. Ears are covered with fur when hamsters are young and become bald with age
- bright, clear eyes
- clean, dry nose and mouth
- clean, undamaged teeth. Check that the front teeth are not too long
- pouches that are in use without any abnormal swellings

If a hamster becomes cold due to a drop in temperature, it will hibernate in a curled-up position and breathe shallowly. It is easy to think that a hibernating hamster has died; however, it will revive slowly in a warm room or held in your hands. In temperatures over 27 degrees celsius, hamsters will overheat and may become rigid and shake for several minutes.

Hamsters can catch colds and influenza; symptoms are sore eyes and nose and sneezing. If you suspect that your pet has a cold, take it to the vet. It is thought that hamsters can catch these infections from humans. You should also visit the vet if your hamster falls, appears shocked and has not recovered after one hour.

BUDGERIGARS

Budgerigars come in a variety of colours.

Many wild birds have been tamed by humans – canaries, parrots, parakeets and cockatiels – but the most popular pet bird is the budgerigar, a member of the parrot family. They are easy to care for and to tame, and they do not require as much room as a cat or a dog.

In their native habitat of Australia, they live in flocks, normally of about 20 birds, although if food and water is scarce, the flocks can be much larger. Buderigars are nomadic, constantly moving on in search of food. Their wild colours of yellow and green offer them some camouflage amongst the shrubs and grass when they are feeding. The hen lays her eggs in a hollow in a tree trunk, the male (cock), helps to rear the young.

The short hooked beak is used for breaking open seeds, the eyes are set on the side of the head, giving a wide field of vision and they have excellent eyesight. The senses of smell and taste are not highly developed. Budgerigars' bones are hollow and they have air spaces in their skulls; this means that their bodies are very light, enabling them to fly. They have four claws on each foot, two facing forwards and two backwards, so they have a strong grip when they are perching.

Budgerigars were first brought to the UK in 1840. Through breeding there are now hundreds of different types. The main differences are in colour and markings; budgerigars can be yellow, green, white, blue, grey, or a mixture of colours.

A healthy pet budgerigar can live for over ten years if it is well cared for, although in the wild they only live for two or three years.

GETTING READY

The cage must be large enough for the budgerigar to fly in; remember that they fly from side to side rather than vertically, so it should be wider that it is tall. It should measure at least 60 x 26 x 26cm and have horizontal bars to enable the bird to climb. The bars should not be any more than 10mm apart. Many cages have sliding trays which make cleaning easier. You should position the cage off the ground, out of the reach of other pets and out of direct sunlight and draughts.

Line the bottom of the cage with paper and a layer of woodshavings or sand; it is possible get special sheets of sand from pet shops. The budgerigar needs something to perch on. Two or three small fruit tree branches wedged between the bars at different heights will enable it to fly from one to the other.

You will also need a birdbath, some small toys and a cover to put over the cage. If your bird is going to live alone, a small mirror will make it feel as though it has some company.

FEEDING
You will need:
- water container
- seed container
- grit container

These should have perches for the bird to stand on whilst eating. Clip them onto the bars of the cage, away from the branches, or they will be soiled with droppings. You will also need a small shallow tray for fresh food.

You also need:
- all-in-one seed mix
- soluble grit
- piece of cuttlefish
- a small iodine block

These need to be stored in airtight containers.

Cleaning equipment
- small cage, for when you are cleaning out the main cage
- rubber gloves
- bucket
- sponge
- detergent
- scrubbing brush
- scraper
- bottle brush
- disinfectant spray (check with the vet which is suitable)
- plant sprayer

CHOOSING A BUDGERIGAR

Budgerigars are sociable birds and will live happily in pairs. The best time to get a budgerigar is July or August, when breeders tend to be sorting out their stock. They can be bought direct from a breeder or a pet shop, or you may find that a local animal shelter has them available. It does not really matter which sex you get; a male and a female are unlikely to breed in your cage as they need special conditions to encourage mating.

Choose young birds as they are easier to tame and train. Budgerigars that are under three months old have black bars on their foreheads; adult birds have plain foreheads and a white ring around their pupils. A young bird should be able to feed itself independently before being taken away from its mother.

Look for a budgerigar that:
- is an alert, active bird
- has bright, clear eyes
- has a smooth, undamaged beak
- has clean feathers; check under the tail
- has undamaged wings
- has a firm grip when perching

GOING HOME

Take your budgerigar home in a secure cardboard box, with holes for ventilation. Put it into the prepared cage and cover it with a cloth to allow it to settle down.

FEEDING

Budgerigars are omnivores; they eat both plants and meat. They will generally feed in the morning and evening.

Put enough food in the seed container to last for the day. When it is almost empty, throw away the remaining food and wash and dry the container thoroughly. Budgerigars need to eat grit as it helps to grind up the seeds in their stomachs, so make sure that the grit container is always full. A piece of cuttlefish clipped to the bars of the cage will give your bird calcium, whilst an iodine block provides extra minerals. Always supply clean, fresh water.

Once a day you can offer the bird some fresh food. Pieces of washed fruit such as apples and pears, and vegetables like carrots and celery should be put on a tray on the floor of the cage. Experiment with different foods to find out what your bird likes.

PREENING

You will see the budgerigar gnawing at its perch; this prevents its beak from growing too long.

The bird will preen itself with its beak to keep clean. It is also spreading an oil from a gland underneath the tail over its feathers; this keeps them waterproof. It will use the bath when necessary.

Once a year budgerigars moult, losing their old feathers and growing new ones. If a bird is kept indoors in fairly constant temperatures, this tends to happen in late spring or early summer when the central heating is turned off and the temperature drops. They tend to lose weight before starting to shed their feathers, and whilst moulting, budgerigars can catch colds. Once they start moulting, they should be fed with seed that has been treated with cod liver oil and allowed plenty of rest.

CLEANING

Every day, remove any dirty wood shavings or sand and replace with clean material. Remove any empty seed shells from the seed container, clean the water container and refill it. Once a week, take the bird out of its cage and put it into the small cage. Whilst it is in there, spray it with water with the plant sprayer to keep its plumage healthy. Make sure that the sprayer is not used for spraying plants with chemicals. Take everything out of the cage and throw away the wood shavings and paper. Wash the trays thoroughly, spray with disinfectant and leave to dry completely before replacing the litter. Wipe the cage bars and spray them with disinfectant. Clean out the food containers, refill them and return them to the cage, along with the cuttlefish and iodine.

HANDLING

It will take a young budgerigar a few weeks to get used to you. Always use calm, slow movements when you are near the cage and talk to it regularly.

Start taming your bird by offering it a piece of food through the bars of the cage, and stroking it gently whilst it is eating. You can then fasten a piece of food onto a perch and encourage the bird to move onto the perch whilst you are holding it. Eventually it will be happy to move onto your hand and perch on your finger. If you need to examine your bird, hold it firmly in cupped hands.

Budgerigars need regular exercise. Once it is tame enough to sit on your finger, it can be taken out of the cage and allowed to fly around the room. Before doing this, make sure the room is safe:

- all doors and windows should be firmly closed
- fireplaces should be screened off to prevent the bird from flying up the chimney
- other pets should not be in the room

Leave the cage open with some fresh food, to tempt the bird back. If it will not return, throw a clean cloth over it, gently scoop it up and put it back in the cage. After exercise, cover the cage and allow the bird to rest. Always cover the cage at night.

BREEDING

Budgerigars need a nesting box if they are to breed. The hen lays between four and six eggs which hatch after about 18 days. The chicks are born blind and without feathers. These start to grow at about 17 days and are soft and downy. By the time the chicks are six weeks old they can feed themselves but cannot yet fly properly. However, they are old enough to leave the mother hen. At four months the chicks moult and grow their adult feathers. Hens are able to lay eggs from about five months of age.

HEALTH

Examine your budgerigar regularly to make sure that it is healthy, looking for the same things that are listed under Choosing a Budgerigar (see p 42). If the appearance or behaviour of your bird changes, take it to the vet.

GOLDFISH

Goldfish are coldwater fish that belong to the minnow family. Unlike tropical fish, they do not require heated tanks; in fact it is possible to keep them in a garden pond where they will grow to a much larger size than those kept in an indoor tank. They normally measure between 8-15cm, although in a pond they may well grow to 30cm.

In their natural habitat fish tend to live in shoals, so goldfish can be kept in the same tank as other coldwater fish. They have a streamlined shape and swim with a side-to-side movement of the rear part of their body. The fins are used to balance and keep them steady in the water. Fish breathe through their gills, taking oxygen from the water.

Goldfish are native to eastern Asia but can be found in freshwater areas around the world. Domestic varieties of goldfish are generally a golden red colour; in their natural habitat they are a dull green. Goldfish were first kept and bred in China during the 5th century. Selective breeding has produced different colourings such as white and silver, and different body shapes. It is thought that goldfish were first introduced to the UK in 1691.

Goldfish are unlikely to breed in your tank as they need special conditions. A goldfish can live for many years, if properly cared for. Some have been said to reach an age of 70 years.

GETTING READY

It is best to buy the largest tank that you can afford. A tank measuring 60cm wide x 15cm high x 12cm deep is large enough for five fish. Obviously, a smaller tank will house fewer fish. A large tank should have a cover or hood containing a lighting unit and be placed on a sturdy piece of furniture or stand. The tank

Goldfish make very popular first pets.

should not be positioned in direct sunlight or near a radiator, and should be out of reach of other pets and young children. Make sure that you are happy with the tank's position before you fill it as it is virtually impossible to move a tank full of water without damaging it.

You will also need:
- a smaller tank, for quarantine or hospital purposes
- electrical pump and filter
- tank thermometer
- bucket thermometer
- water conditioner
- water quality testing kit
- gravel
- pebbles and small rocks (not limestone)
- underwater plants

Ask an adult to fit the electrical equipment and do not plug it in until you have set up the rest of your tank. The gravel should be bought from a pet shop or aquarist shop; wash it in the sieve until the water is clear. Position the gravel so that it slopes gently down to the front of the tank; this allows food and fish waste to collect at the front and makes it easier to clean.

Tap water contains chlorine which can make your fish ill. It is possible to buy water conditioner which makes the water suitable for goldfish – follow the instructions carefully. If you do not use conditioner, you will need to leave the water for several days before putting in any fish, to allow the chlorine to evaporate. Half-fill the tank with water. Always pour water onto a small plate placed in the tank so that it does not disturb the gravel.

Arrange the pebbles and rocks so that they provide some hiding places for the fish. Plants give the fish shelter and also release oxygen into the water. Make sure they look healthy and place them in the gravel. Fill the tank to within 5cm of the top with conditioned water.

Fix the thermometer to the inside of the tank with rubber suction cups, making sure it is in a position where it is easy to read. Switch on the pump and lighting unit. The pump should always be left running, the light should be turned on in the morning and off at night.

Check the tank when you switch on the lighting unit in the morning. Make sure that the filter is working and the water is clean. The temperature should remain steady on the thermometer, at about 18 degrees celsius. For the first two weeks after you set up your tank, use the water quality testing kit to check the level of nitrates.

Cleaning equipment:
- bucket
- siphon
- magnetic glass cleaner
- scraper
- cloth
- brush
- sieve
- net

CHOOSING GOLDFISH

If you are going to keep a number of fish it is best not to put them all in the tank at the same time. Buying two fish every other week would allow the bacteria that develops in the tank and kills harmful fish waste time to develop. If you plan to keep other types of fish with your goldfish, ask in an aquarist shop or a fish breeders club for advice.

Look for fish that:
- are kept in clean tanks
- are active
- have bright, shiny skin
- have upright, undamaged fins.

GOING HOME

The fish can be transported in a plastic bag half-filled with water. Ask whether they have been quarantined. If not, you can do this yourself.

It is important that your new fish are not put directly from the bag into the tank, as the sudden change in temperature could be harmful. Float the bag unopened in the tank for about 20 minutes. Open the bag and gently pour small quantities of water from the tank into it. Using a small net, guide the fish from the bag into the tank.

FEEDING

Your goldfish will nibble at some of the plants and the algae that grows on the inside of the tank. You should feed them with dried fish food in the morning and evening; they only need a very small pinch of food, scattered onto the surface of the water.

You can also buy frozen, dried or live fresh food. Give this to your fish once a week. If the fish are eating the plants, you can give them a lettuce leaf once a week. Dip it in boiling water and allow it to cool before floating it on the surface. Remove it after 12 hours.

It is possible to buy special food tablets for when you are going to be away on holiday. Do not overfeed your fish, as the water will become dirty and make them ill.

CLEANING

Generally the water will need partially changing every two weeks, however you should also change it if the nitrate level is too high or the water looks cloudy.

Switch off and unplug the electrical equipment. Take the hood off the tank and wipe it with a damp cloth. Using the siphon, take about ten percent of water out of the tank into a bucket. If you move the siphon over the gravel at the front of the tank, this will remove any fish waste that has collected there.

Cut back any plants that are becoming too big. Scrape off algae from the front and sides of the tank; it can be left on the back of the tank as it provides food for the fish. Use the magnetic cleaner to clean the glass. Wash the filter and rinse the sponges. Siphon another ten percent of water from the tank to remove any algae or plant cuttings left in the water.

Prepare some water in a bucket by adding conditioner. Do not add this water until it is the same temperature as the water in the tank. Remember to pour it onto a plate so that it does not disturb the fish.

HEALTH

If one of your goldfish starts to behave differently, take it out of the main tank and put it into a separate quarantine tank until it appears to have returned to normal. If it does not appear to be recovering, talk to a vet or aquarist. A quarantine tank should be prepared in much the same way as a normal tank, although plants and pebbles are not necessary.

When you buy new fish, they should be kept in a quarantine tank for about two weeks, unless you are told that they have already been quarantined. This ensures they will not spread illness and infection to your other fish.

Sometimes fish will attack each other. If their skin is damaged they may develop a fungal infection. You will see a white growth on their bodies. Put the fish into a quarantine tank, adding a teaspoonful of sea salt for every litre of water.

If you notice small white spots on your fish's skin, put the affected fish into a quarantine tank. Ask an aquarist for chemicals to treat the condition.

Fin-rot is a result of fish damaging their fins; again an aquarist will advise you on available chemicals.

CHAMELEONS

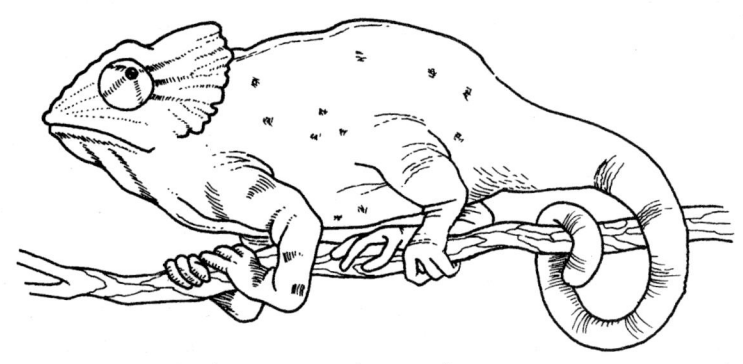

Chameleons make fascinating and unusual pets.

Chameleons are reptiles belonging to the *iguanidae* family. The correct name for them is 'anoles', and they were in existence during the Jurassic period, about 130 million years ago.

There are over 80 species of chameleon. In the wild, they live in tropical areas and can be found in Africa, Madagascar, Europe and Asia. They are diurnal creatures, waking as the sun rises and sleeping during the hours of darkness. They spend the daylight hours resting among the leaves of shrubs and trees and searching for food. They eat insects, moving slowly in on them and then darting out their extremely long, sticky tongues to catch them. They will also eat young lizards.

Chameleons are well known for their ability to change colour. This colour change is caused by hormones that affect colour cells in the skin and is generally due to changes in light and temperature. A chameleon will also change colour if it is frightened, but not as a camouflage technique as is commonly thought. The American chameleon is green in colour; when it is asleep it is generally a pale brown, with a white underside. If it is frightened it turns brown all over and will become grey or yellow if it is cold.

Chameleons vary in size, depending on the species. They range from a few centimetres in length to around 40cm. They have divided toes which they use to hold on to branches when climbing; they can also use their tails for grasping. The tail of a chameleon is also used for balance when climbing; however, if it is grasped by a predator, it will break off. The chameleon uses this as a means of escaping from its enemies and has the ability to grow another tail.

A chameleon cannot turn its short neck; instead it moves its eyes independently from each other in all directions, giving it a wide range of vision. Its body is a flattened shape on the sides and the skin is rough and covered in scales. Some males have horned heads, which they sometimes use for fighting.

GETTING READY

A large glass tank or aquarium, known as a vivarium, makes an ideal home for a chameleon. A tank measuring at least 30cm x 20cm x 20cm will house two medium-sized chameleons. It will need a secure, well-ventilated lid as chameleons can climb up the glass sides. An aquarium lid containing a lighting unit would be suitable.

You will need:
- gravel or small pebbles
- charcoal chips
- sandy soil
- plants
- branches
- thermometer

The vivarium should be kept in a warm place but out of direct sunlight. Chameleons are cold-blooded; their body temperature depends on their environment and they should be kept at a constant temperature of between 24 and 30 degrees celsius. You need to get a heating unit from a pet shop. Background heating and a basking spot with thermostats is also required. Ask an adult to fit and connect this for you.

Make the inside of the vivarium as much like the chameleon's natural environment as possible. Spread 2.5cm of gravel or small pebbles over the bottom of the tank, covered with a thin layer of charcoal chips to absorb smells and help to keep the soil sweet. Spread 2.5cm of soil on top of the charcoal.

Put in a few branches for the chameleon to climb, positioned so that your pet can hide underneath them. Plants also provide shelter; keep them in their pots rather than planting them, as this makes it easier when you are cleaning out the vivarium.

Cleaning equipment:
- plastic container with secure ventilated lid
- small plastic spade
- bucket
- cloth

CHOOSING A CHAMELEON

A pet shop may stock chameleons or be able to give you some advice on where to get them from.

It is difficult to keep more than one chameleon as, unless they are a similar size, the larger chameleon will eat the smaller one. Male chameleons tend to fight in defence of their territory and females.

Look for a chameleon that:
- is being kept in a clean vivarium
- is young and wary of you
- has undamaged skin, feet and claws

GOING HOME

Transport your chameleon in a secure, ventilated container. Make sure it is not left in direct sunlight.

FEEDING

A chameleon will eat about 24 insects a week. They will eat virtually any moving insect: houseflies, small grasshoppers, beetles and spiders. Do not give your chameleon moths as it could choke on the powder that covers the moth's body. It is possible to buy mealworms or crickets from pet shops; these should be put into a shallow container in the vivarium. Try to offer your pet a variety of insects, making sure that they are not contaminated by insecticides.

You can also try feeding it on mashed fruit such as banana, apples and melon and small pieces of raw minced beef. You can train chameleons to feed from your hand as long as you move slowly and calmly and do not alarm them.

Spray the plants in the vivarium with water every day. Chameleons will drink these droplets rather than taking water from a dish.

CLEANING

The vivarium will need cleaning thoroughly every two weeks. Place the chameleon in a secure container, making sure that there are ventilation holes in the lid. Switch off and unplug the lighting unit; clean the lid with a dampened cloth. Take the plants out, water them and remove any branches. Using the plastic spade, take out the top layer of soil and charcoal chips; this should be thrown away. Put the pebbles into a strong bucket filled with water. Rinse them until the water runs clear, then dry the pebbles very thoroughly as chameleons do not like excessive moisture.

Clean the vivarium floor and sides with a damp cloth; the chameleons will be less likely to climb to the top as they find it hard to hold on to clean glass. Replace the dry pebbles and the layers of fresh charcoal chips, soil and branches. Arrange the plants, ensuring they are well drained, and finally return the chameleons to the vivarium.

BREEDING

The best way to identify male and female chameleons is by their fan; a large fold of skin. A male's fan is

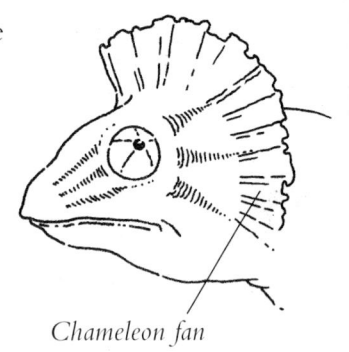

Chameleon fan

larger and more brightly coloured than that of a female. Male chameleons will display their fans if they are feeling defensive. Holding a mirror in front of a chameleon so that it can see its reflection will cause it to display its fan.

A male will usually mate with one female each season – in fact, he might keep the same mate for several seasons. If a female lays eggs in the vivarium, take them out and put them between moist paper towels or bury them under about 1cm of moist peat or decayed wood. The eggs need to be kept warm. Spray the surface of the paper or litter occasionally to keep them damp. If the eggs are left in the vivarium, they, and any young that hatch, will be eaten by adult chameleons. A female lays between one and three small soft-shelled eggs. Young chameleons are born measuring about 5cm in length, they are fully formed and completely independent.

HEALTH

Check your chameleon regularly to make sure it has not been injured in any way. Pay particular attention to the skin, feet and nose. Reptiles do tend to rub their noses against transparent objects, which can cause them to become infected.

If your pet's appearance, appetite or behaviour changes at all, take it to the vet.

STICK INSECTS

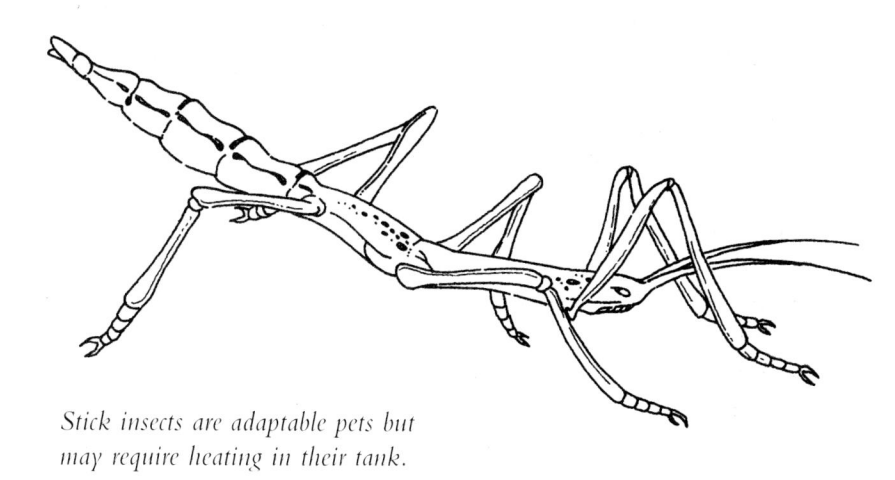

Stick insects are adaptable pets but may require heating in their tank.

Stick insects make interesting pets. They do not take up a lot of space and will breed easily in captivity.

They can be found in the wild in India, Indonesia, Australia, Malaysia, Central and Southern America and Africa. Two species of stick insects have been introduced to the south west of the UK; in the Scilly Isles, Devon and Cornwall, where the climate is fairly mild.

Stick insects are, as their name suggests, twig-like in shape. Some species can change colour to blend in with their surroundings. They are very agile, having claws and sucker pads on their feet, and can hang upside down and walk up the sides of a glass tank.

A stick insect's body is in three parts: the head with two antennae; the thorax, (which is in three segments, each having a pair of legs attached); and the abdomen. The legs also have three parts and are fragile and easily damaged. Some species have sharp spikes on their legs which can be painful if the stick insect digs them into your skin.

Although some species have wings, there are very few that can actually fly. A small number of species can produce a chemical spray from glands near the head. This is a form of defence and if it enters your eyes they can be painful for a couple of days.

GETTING READY

An aquarium makes an ideal home for stick insects. It will need a fine mesh lid, to keep the insects inside the tank (known as a vivarium), and yet allow ventilation. It should be large enough to allow the stick insects to moult; they do this whilst hanging upside down from a twig, so it needs to be at least twice as high as the length of the insects.

As stick insects come from warm climates, they may require some form of heating. It is possible to buy heating pads, which are placed underneath the tank, from pet shops.

You will need:
- newspaper or white paper
- dry twigs
- peat
- piece of bark
- sphagnum moss
- plant sprayer

Line the floor with a layer of paper. Although you can use newspaper, white paper is useful for spotting the stick insect's eggs. Most species will stay on the plants that you provide for food, others – such as the Giant Spiny – will spend time on the floor and will need some cover, so some peat or a piece of bark will provide shelter. Put a pile of sphagnum moss in one corner; spray this regularly with water to increase the humidity. Supply a number of twigs for the stick insects to climb.

CHOOSING A STICK INSECT

Pet shops do not necessarily stock stick insects, although they may be able to get hold of them for you. Otherwise, contact the Phasmid Study Group (see Useful Addresses, p 63).

It is best to buy young stick insects (nymphs) once they have moulted, or shed their skin, a few times. They are able to regrow any missing limbs, unlike older insects. Also, adult insects may only live for a few weeks or months after you have got them.

Look for a stick insect that:
- does not have a twisted body, as this could make moulting difficult
- does not have any limbs missing

Find out whether you are getting a species that requires heating in their tank and what their eating habits are. Avoid those that will only eat one plant, as it may be difficult to get hold of.

GOING HOME

Transport your stick insects in a plastic box with a lid, making sure there are ventilation holes in the box. Place some plant food in the box and keep it out of direct sunlight during the journey.

FEEDING

Stick insects appear to adapt quite readily to different diets. Most species will eat bramble (blackberry) leaves. Always collect these from areas that you are certain have not been sprayed with chemicals and away from roadsides, where they may have been polluted by car exhaust fumes.

Always pick green leaves and check the undersides for insect eggs, removing any leaves that are soiled with bird droppings. Leave the leaves on the stems rather than picking them off and rinse them under cold water; the insects will drink the water droplets. You may find that your insects will also eat privet, ivy, rose and oak leaves.

Stick insects need a constant supply of food. Cut the bramble to a length that will fit into the vivarium, make a vertical slit, about 1cm deep, in the base of the stem. Place the bramble in a narrow-necked container filled with water, making sure that the container will not tip over with the weight of the insects. Plug the neck with cotton wool or tissue to prevent any insects from falling in and drowning and put the container into the vivarium.

Once you are used to the amount of food that your insects need, it is easier to judge the amount of bramble you should give them. It should last two or three days before starting to wilt.

If you have a species of stick insect that drinks, put a small amount of water in a shallow dish on the floor of the tank. The lid of a coffee jar is a suitable container; do not fill it to the top or your insects may drown in it.

Tropical species need higher humidity, so spray the inside of the vivarium lightly with water twice a day.

MOULTING

Nymphs shed their skin a number of times before reaching adulthood. The number of moults depends on the species and the temperature, but on average it will happen five or six times. Higher temperatures lead to an increased number of moults.

Prior to a moult happening, the insect tends to be less active and may lose its appetite for a couple of days. It will hang upside down from a twig and the skin will split in a straight line along the top of the thorax. The head of the insect emerges first and, after a rest, the remainder of the body. It is easy to see an increase in size. The stick insect will stay still for a couple of hours whilst the new skin hardens. It is important not to handle them at this stage as they can be easily injured.

Males live for about one month after their final moult, females can live for up to six months. As the insects age they need more water; they eventually become less active and finally die and fall to the floor.

HANDLING

Treat your stick insects very gently. Once they are used to you, they will walk on to your hand, but do not make any sudden movements and always hold your other hand beneath them in case they fall.

If you do need to pick them up, place your finger and thumb on either side of the thorax, avoiding the legs. Try not to pull them off the plants as they may damage their legs.

CLEANING

The paper floor covering needs to be changed twice a week; you should be able to do this without disturbing your pets.

Once a month clean the vivarium thoroughly. Remove all of the insects and place them in a secure, ventilated container. Take out the dry twigs and plant food, checking for insect eggs and nymphs. Wash the tank and dry it thoroughly before replacing the contents.

BREEDING

Female stick insects tend to be larger than the males; the rear end of their abdomen is pointed, whereas in the male it is square. All species reproduce by means of eggs; however, some are able to breed without mating. These are known as parthenogenetic.

Some females scatter their eggs anywhere, others hide their eggs or bury them. If this is the case you will need to provide a small pot containing sand or peat. The Pink-winged female lays her eggs underneath leaves. The Giant Prickly stick insect can produce up to 1000 eggs; parthenogenetic females tend to lay fewer.

Stick insects' eggs vary in size and appearance. Some look like the seeds of plants, which protects them from enemies in the wild. Eggs can take from two months to one year to hatch, so it is advisable to remove them from the vivarium. They seem to hatch faster if kept at a temperature of 21 to 29 degrees celsius and are not allowed to dry out.

When the nymphs hatch they look like mini versions of the adult, although they do not have wings. Put some food close by, do not handle them and keep them at a temperature of 24 degrees celsius.

As the nymphs grow they will need to be separated into smaller groups. If you notice that they are suffering from damaged legs, this could indicate that they are overcrowded.

HEALTH

If a stick insect loses a limb it may develop a fungal infection. This is very difficult to cure and it is probably kinder to kill the insect. Placing it in a box in the deep freeze appears to be the best form of euthanasia in this case.

If a number of your insects die, check that the food supply is not polluted. Collect the leaves from a different location to see if this solves the problem. Also check the levels of humidity in the vivarium. Keep it out of direct sunlight as this will kill your pets. Remember that insecticides will kill. Do not use fly spray in the same room as the vivarium and preferably not in the house at all.

USEFUL ADDRESSES

RSPCA
The Manor House
Horsham
West Sussex
RH12 1HG

The Kennel Club
1 Clarges St
London W1

The National Cavy Club
9 Parkdale Rd
Sheldon
Birmingham
B26 3UT

The Budgerigar Society
49/53 Hazelwood Rd
Northampton
NN1 1LG

Federation of British Aquatic Societies
18 The Barons
St Margarets
Twickenham
Middlesex

The Phasmid Study Group
(Stick insects)
'Papillon'
40 Thorndike Rd
Slough
Berkshire
SL2 1SR

INDEX

Ark (see Mordant run)

Bedding,
　cats 12
　dogs 5

Behaviour,
　cats 16

Breeding,
　budgerigars 45
　cats 16
　chameleons 56
　dogs 10
　guinea pigs 31
　hamsters 38
　rabbits 24
　stick insects 61

Cages,
　budgerigars 41
　hamsters 34, 35

Cat flap 13

Choosing,
　budgerigars 42
　cats 13
　chameleons 54
　dogs 6
　goldfish 49
　guinea pigs 28
　hamsters 36
　rabbits 21
　stick insects 59

Cleaning,
　budgerigar cages 44
　chameleon tanks 55
　goldfish tanks 49
　guinea pig hutches 30
　hamster cages 37
　rabbit hutches 23
　stick insect tanks 61

Cleaning equipment,
　budgerigars 42
　chameleons 54
　goldfish 49
　guinea pigs 28
　hamsters 37
　rabbits 20
　stick insects 61

Collar and lead 6, 8

Exercise, dogs 4

Feeding,
　budgerigars 43
　cats 15
　chameleons 55
　dogs 8
　goldfish 50
　guinea pigs 29
　hamsters 36
　rabbits 22, *22*
　stick insects 59

Feeding equipment,
　budgerigars 41
　cats 13
　dogs 5
　guinea pigs 28
　hamsters 36
　rabbits 20

Grooming,
　cats 15
　dogs 9
　guinea pigs 30
　hamsters 37
　rabbits 23

Grooming equipment,
　cats 13
　dogs 5
　guinea pigs 28
　rabbits 20, 21

Handling,
　budgerigars 44
　guinea pigs 30, *30*
　hamsters 38

Health,
　budgerigars 45
　cats 17
　chameleons 56
　dogs 10
　goldfish 51
　guinea pigs 32
　hamsters 39
　rabbits 25
　stick insects 62

House-training,
　cats 14
　dogs 7

Hutches,
　guinea pigs 27, *27*
　rabbits 19, *19*

Identity disc 6

Injections (see vaccinations)

Litter tray 12

Mordant run 21, *21*, 27

Moulting,
　budgerigars 44
　stick insects 60

Neutering,
　cats 16
　dogs 10

Preening 44

Tank,
　chameleons 53
　goldfish 46
　stick insects 58

Training, dogs 8

Vaccinations,
　cats 14
　dogs 6